For

_____,

An Officially Excellent Friend

_____

from

_____

date

OUR PURPOSE AT HOWARD PUBLISHING IS TO:

- *Increase faith* in the hearts of growing Christians
- *Inspire holiness* in the lives of believers
- *Instill hope* in the hearts of struggling people everywhere

BECAUSE HE'S COMING AGAIN!

Published by Howard Publishing Co., Inc.
3117 North 7th Street, West Monroe, Louisiana 71291-2227

03 04 05 06 07 08 09 10 11 12   10 9 8 7 6 5 4 3 2 1

Edited by Between the Lines
Interior design by Stephanie Denney
Illustrations by Kristy Caldwell
Cover design by LinDee Loveland

ISBN: 1-58229-307-4 ; 1-58229-319-8 (pbk)

The Who, What, When, Where, Why, and How of **Friendship**

THE "official" friends BOOK

Martha Bolton

HOWARD
PUBLISHING CO.

Illustrated by
Kristy Caldwell

The world is a nicer place because of friends.

Contents
❀

Friends! Where would we be without them?

I have never met a person whose greatest need was anything other than real, unconditional love.

Elizabeth Kubler-Ross

Friendship

Friends—where would any of us be without them? Whether it's the familiar voice on the other end of the telephone, the periodic e-mail that appears in our mailbox—the one we open first, before spending the next twenty minutes deleting junk mail—or the unexpected card that comes just when we need it most; friends brighten our days.

From the first "best" friend we had in kindergarten to the many relationships we've added to our lives since, friends play a major role in our development. They laugh with us, cry with us, encourage us, listen to us, advise us, defend us, and gently challenge us to be better people.

Not everyone we meet will become a friend. Not everyone we call *friend* will prove to be a true one. But for those who have stood the test of time, who've proven over and over again to be friends we can count on in both good times and in bad, this book is a way of saying thank you: The world is a nicer place for all of us because of friends like you.

Friends play a major role in our development.

If one falls down,
his friend can help him up.
But pity the man who falls and
has no one to help him up!

—Ecclesiastes 4:10

Friendship

Friends care whether or not you've had a nice day.

THE who OF friendship

A friend is someone with whom you dare to be yourself.

Frank Crane

A true friend is someone who thinks that you are a good egg even though he knows that you are slightly cracked.

Bernard Meltzer

Friends Like Us

A friend is more than a name we jot down in an address book and years later forget who she is or where we met her. A friend is more than a screen name on Instant Messaging or someone we nod to as we pass by. A friend is not a door-to-door salesman who needs you to be his tenth customer so he can win a trip to the Bahamas. She's not someone who tells you halfheartedly to have a nice day, then never sees you again to find out whether you did. A friend isn't someone who calls when he needs a favor, then doesn't return your phone call when you need one.

A friend is much more than that.

Friends want to be with us whether we can do anything for them or not. They're not interested in our money or our influence. They won't use us or abuse the relationship. Friends care whether or not you've had a nice day. To paraphrase the immortal words of Sally Field at the Academy Awards, "They like us; they really, really like us!" No strings attached. No ulterior motives. No games. No phoniness. Just honest friendship. That's who a real friend is.

Friends like us; they really like us.

How Can You Tell
Who Your Friends Are?

Friends tell
each other
about 50-percent-off sales.

Friends never brag or gloat,
even if their children
or grandchildren really are
the cutest in the world.

**Friends laugh together.
Often.**

Friends don't feel pressured to fill every silence with trivial chatter. They're comfortable just being in each other's company.

Friends can call each other any
time of the day or night.

**Friends hurt
when friends hurt.**

Friends don't remember who paid for lunch last time, but it always seems to come out even.

When a friend sends a postcard that
says, "Wish you were here,"
she really, really
wishes you were.

Friends know us well enough to finish our sentences—but value our input enough to let us speak.

Friends share the last brownie on the plate.

Oh the comfort, the inexpressible comfort of feeling safe

with a person, having neither to weigh thoughts

nor measure words, but pouring them all right out,

just as they are—chaff and grain together—

certain that a faithful hand will take and sift them,

keep what is worth keeping,

and with the breath of kindness blow the rest away.

Dinah Mulock

> **Friends are those rare people who ask how we are
> and then wait to hear the answer.**

Ed Cunningham

Friends Hear Us

Have you ever had this happen to you? Someone asks how you're doing, but before you can get out the news that your husband was taken to the hospital last week with chest pains, your daughter was expelled from school again, and your mother's cancer has returned, they've already moved on to their crisis of the moment—that the grocery store ran out of the baked beans that were advertised.

Some people don't see very far beyond their own lives, do they?

True friends aren't like that. True friends ask how you're doing and care about your answer. They listen when you tell them about your day, your week, and your life. They read between the lines. They hear more than what you're saying, not less. They want to know if your husband is getting the right medical treatment and if they can do anything to help your daughter or mother. They're already praying for you before you even finish telling them about your week.

To a real friend, "How are you?" is more than a casual greeting. It's an invitation to open up, to share what's on your heart, to trust that what you say will fall on a caring ear—and a confidential one. To a friend, "How are you?" is an unspoken offer of help and a quiet but steady reassurance of love and concern.

To a real friend, "How are you?" is more than a casual greeting.

The friend in my adversity I shall always cherish most.

I can better trust those who helped to relieve the gloom

of my dark hours than those who are

so ready to enjoy with me

the sunshine of my prosperity.

Ulysses S. Grant

My best friend is the one who brings out the best in me.

Henry Ford

Friends Build Us

True friends don't see our shortcomings, because our potential blinds them. They don't waste time pointing out the worst in us. They put their energies into bringing out the best. Instead of seeing our failures, they see all the successes waiting for us just around the corner. They don't focus on how much we need to improve. They focus on how much good is already in us. They encourage us to achieve what we didn't even realize we were capable of achieving. They inspire us. No matter how much we accomplish in life or where

> *Some friends don't help, but a true friend is closer than your own family.*
> —Proverbs 18:24 CEV

our journey takes us, true friends have been—and always will be—an important part of our foundation. They build our confidence and self-esteem. They reinforce our inner strength. They support our natural talents. In other words, true friends don't run a wrecking company. They're in the construction business.

True friends see all the successes waiting for us around the corner.

A best friend is like a four leaf clover—
hard to find and lucky to have.

Anonymous

In poverty and other misfortunes of life,
true friends are a sure refuge.
The young they keep out of mischief;
to the old they are a comfort and aid in their weakness;
and those in the prime of life they incite to noble deeds.

Aristotle

To mean something to somebody
is one of the greatest satisfactions in life.

Validivar

What a Friend

What a Friend we have in Jesus,
All our sins and griefs to bear!
What a privilege to carry
Everything to God in pray'r!
O what peace we often forfeit,
O what needless pain we bear,
All because we do not carry
Everything to God in pray'r!

Joseph M. Scriven

The dearest friend on earth
is a mere shadow compared to Jesus Christ.

Oswald Chambers

A friend is someone
who sees through you
and still enjoys the view.

Wilma Askinas

Friendship is wishing nothing but the best for each other.

THE what OF friendship

Friends go to the mat for each other.

The better part of one's life consists of his friendships.

Abraham Lincoln

What a Friend Is

According to the dictionary, friendship is "an attachment to a person arising from mutual esteem and goodwill." That's a pretty accurate assessment of friendship, isn't it?

Unfortunately, it's also where so many of us get it wrong.

Mutual esteem means respecting the opinions of others, not merely putting up with them. It means supporting their dreams, not holding them back because we fear they might leave us behind. It's wishing nothing but the best for them—and knowing they're wishing the same for us.

Friendship is truth, not a performance. It means that everything we say about our friends, both to their faces and behind their backs, is suitable to be written into a speech and delivered at their Man- or Woman-of-the-Year dinner.

Friends also go to the mat for each other. They take you at your word and give you the benefit of the doubt. They not only forgive you when you mess up, but they understand why you did what you did.

Friendship isn't a part-time job. Friends are there for us 24/7, encouraging us when we're down, laughing with us when they know we could use a good laugh, and standing by us when everyone else walks away. Friendship is unselfish. It endures. And above all else, it's real.

Friends are there for us 24/7.

Friendships are fragile things

and require as much care in handling

as any other fragile and precious thing.

Randolph S. Bourne

Of all things which wisdom provides to make life entirely happy,

much the greatest is the possession of friendship.

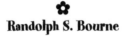

Epicurus

What a Friend Has

Friends have PERFECT TIMING.

They always show up at just the right moment.

Friends have BROAD SHOULDERS.

They're the perfect size for leaning on, crying on, and standing alongside.

Friends have SELECTIVE MEMORIES.

They remember your worth and forget your failures.

Friends have A LIMITED VOCABULARY.

They don't know any discouraging words.

Friends have LONG ARMS.

They can reach down and lift you up,
no matter how far you fall.

Friends have PERFECT VISION.

They can see your best side even when you're not showing it.

Friends have EXCELLENT HEARING.

They hear the love behind your words.

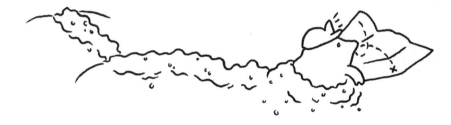

Friends have GREAT ENDURANCE.

They always go the extra mile for you.

Friends have TREMENDOUS STRENGTH.

No burden is too heavy for them to share.

Friends have BIG HEARTS.

They never run out of love.

There is an electricity about a friendship relationship.

We are both more relaxed and more sensitive,

more creative and more reflective,

more energetic and more casual,

more excited and more serene.

Andrew M. Greeley

> From quiet homes and first beginning, out to the
> undiscovered ends, there's nothing worth the wear of
> winning, but laughter and the love of friends.

Hilaire Belloc

Cheerleaders in the Race of Life

If you've ever competed in a race, you know the difference it makes to have friends standing on the sidelines, cheering you on. (I also like to have a couple of paramedics on the sidelines when I run, but that's just me.)

No matter where they've positioned themselves along the path, encouraging friends are always a welcome sight.

"Come on! You can do it!"

"You're almost there! Don't give up now!"

"You're doing great! You're going to make it!"

Few things are more powerful than encouraging words spoken by people who believe in you. And sometimes that's exactly what you need to make it across the finish line.

Just as friends can help us win a physical race, they can also help us win the race of life. We all need friends who will stand on the sidelines, cheering us on to bigger and better accomplishments. We need their encouragement to stay in the race—to believe in ourselves.

"Come on! You can do it!"

Friend

❀

F—fun, forgiving, faithful

R—reliable, real, reassuring

I—inseparable, interested, inspiring

E—encouraging, edifying, energizing

N—nurturing, necessary, noncompetitive

D—dependable, defending, devout

A friend is a present you give to yourself.

Robert Louis Stevenson

Each friend represents a world in us,
a world possibly not born until they arrive,
and it is only by this meeting that a new world is born.

Anais Nin

Friendship is the golden thread that ties the heart of all the world.

John Evelyn

I would rather have a million friends
than a million dollars.

Eddie Rickenbacker

Estimated Worth of a Friend

Counselor

$75 PER HOUR

A friend listens when you need to talk. She helps you process the ups and downs of life. She's not judgmental or controlling. A friend will listen for as long as you need to talk. And if she gives advice, you can count on it coming from an unselfish place. A true friend wants the best for you 100 percent of the time.

*A friend will listen
for as long as you need to talk.*

She will tell you when you're making a huge fashion faux pas.

Fashion Designer
$40 PER HOUR

A friend will take you aside and tell you privately when you're making a huge fashion faux pas. She won't humiliate or belittle you in front of others. She understands that whatever you wear is ultimately your choice. But if you ask, she'll kindly tell you that the ostrich leather jumpsuit has to go.

Secretary

$15 PER HOUR

A friend reminds you of important dates. She doesn't have to. She just wants to. She'll remember your birthday (even if you're trying to forget), your anniversary (even when your spouse forgets), and a host of other landmark occasions in your life. A friend is a walking Palm Pilot that never needs charging and is always ready to "do lunch."

A friend is a walking Palm Pilot.

Friends make exercise (or avoiding it) a lot more fun.

Personal Trainer

$50 PER HOUR

A friend will walk with you, jog with you, bowl with you, or just sit and rock in a rocking chair with you. It doesn't matter if you're burning up five hundred calories in a triathlon or thirty-five calories just laughing together—friends make exercise (or avoiding exercise) a lot more fun.

Nurse

$40 PER HOUR

A friend will help remind you to take your medicine, to get enough rest, to have an annual mammogram or PSA test. She'll tell you when you're working too hard or when you need to reassess your priorities. A friend will tell you that you need to learn to say no, that you're worth more than you might be settling for, and that you're long overdue for a vacation. Friends do all this for selfish reasons—they want to have you around for many more years!

A friend will tell you when you're long overdue for a vacation.

He wants you to graduate from life with high honors.

Teacher

$40 PER HOUR

If you listen, a friend can save you from learning a lot of lessons the hard way. True friends want to do everything they can to help you succeed. They don't want to see you fail or be held back. They don't want to see you hurt. They believe in you. They want you to graduate from this life with the highest honors you're capable of earning.

A faithful friend is the best defense attorney you can have.

Defense Attorney

$200 PER HOUR

A faithful friend is the best defense attorney you can have. Friends stand up for you. They believe in you no matter what accusations are flying. They won't sell you out. They won't defend you one minute, then volunteer to be a witness for the prosecution the next. True friends are loyal. They can't be bought off, intimidated, or swayed. They know the real you. When you need them, you don't have to worry about not being able to find them. They'll be right there, ready, willing, and able to defend you.

Estimated worth of a friend: Priceless

Every man rejoices twice when he has a partner in his joy.

He who shares tears with us, wipes them away.

He divides them in two,

and he who laughs with us makes the joy double.

Bishop Fulton J. Sheen

My friends are my estate.

Emily Dickinson

It takes a lot of time, understanding,
and trust to gain a close friendship with someone.
My friends are my most precious asset.

Erynn Miller

Friendship is the source of the greatest pleasures,
and without friends even the most agreeable pursuits become tedious.

Saint Thomas Aquinas

The ornament of a house is the friends who frequent it.

Ralph Waldo Emerson

Friends are friends from the very start.

THE when OF friendship

A friend's voice is always a welcome sound.

A true friend is forever a friend.

George MacDonald

Any Time Is a Good Time

None of us enjoys having to get out of the shower, crawl out of bed, or leave our favorite TV show just to answer a telephone call from some telemarketer, political action committee, or a solicitor trying to raise funds for the Save the Gnat Society.

But a friend's voice is always a welcome sound, no matter what we're in the middle of doing or what time of the day or night it happens to be. As soon as we hear that familiar voice or recognize that telephone number on our Caller ID, we gladly give ourselves permission to take a break from our mundane tasks. Why? Because friends renew us. Just when we're feeling as though things can't possibly get any worse, our friends come along and remind us of our inner strength. They renew our resolve. They allow us to vent about the frustrations of our day, and before we know it, they have us laughing again. Friends make life just a little easier every minute of every day.

It's the ones you can call up at 4 A.M. that really matter.

Marlene Dietrich

I value the friend who for me finds time on his calendar,
but I cherish the friend who for me does not consult his calendar.

Robert Brault

Friends take time for each other. They understand the importance of making new memories and building on old ones. They take time to laugh, to listen, to share, to be vulnerable, to reaffirm, to encourage, and to grow a deeper friendship. True friends—and true friendships—take time.

Friendship is a plant of slow growth and must undergo and withstand the shocks of adversity before it is entitled to the appellation.

George Washington

I still find each day too short for all the thoughts I want to think,
all the walks I want to take, all the books I want to read,
and all the friends I want to see.

John Burrough

Come the wild weather, come sleet or come snow,
we will stand by each other, however it blow.

Simon Dach

A Friend Loves at All Times

W<small>HEN DARK CLOUDS COME</small>,
a friend doesn't run.

WHEN YOU'RE DROWNING IN A FLOOD OF TROUBLES,
a friend doesn't swim away.

WHEN A SITUATION GETS TOO HOT TO BEAR,
a friend gets out a fan and bears it with you.

WHEN THE WINDS OF CHANGE ARE BLOWING,
a friend helps you stand up in the midst of them.

WHEN YOU FIND YOURSELF IN HOT WATER,
**a friend shows up just in time
to help cool things down.**

WHEN THINGS GET A LITTLE STICKY,

a friend doesn't leave you stuck.

WHEN YOU NEED A WARM HUG,
a friend won't give you the cold shoulder.

WHEN YOU MAKE A MISTAKE,
a friend doesn't get hot under the collar.

WHEN YOU FEEL LIKE YOU'RE IN A FOG,
a friend will help you see more clearly.

WHEN THE WORLD FEELS COLD AND GLOOMY,
a friend will be your sunshine.

> **A real friend is one who walks in
> when the rest of the world walks out.**
>
>
>
> **Walter Winchell**

True friends are evergreens. They don't thrive in the springs and summers of our lives only to turn dormant when the autumns and winters roll around. They can be counted on year 'round, through every season, no matter how hard the winds blow or how much rain falls. And when the good weather returns once again—and it will—they will be by our side to rejoice with us.

True friends are evergreens.

Perfect Timing

Friends have a knack for showing up

...just when your back is against the wall.

...just when you need someone to talk to.

...just when you're feeling all alone.

...just when nothing seems to be going right.

...just when you're ready to give up.

...just when you think nobody cares.

Friends have a knack for showing up
at just the right moment.

In prosperity our friends know us;
in adversity we know our friends.

John Churton Collins

Friends Don't...

...need an invitation. They know exactly when to show up and what to do when they get there.

...waver. A true friend stays by your side regardless of whether you're on top of the world or down on your luck.

A friend loves at all times.

—Proverbs 17:17

...wear two faces. They're the same friend in front of you as they are behind your back.

...leave when the going gets tough. They're 100 percent committed to the friendship.

**A friend hears the song in my heart and sings
it to me when my memory fails.**

Anonymous

Friends Always Know Just What to Do

When you drop your soda on the floor in the middle of the mall, a friend will not only help you clean it up but will offer to share hers or get you another one.

When you say or do something stupid, a friend will say it wasn't as dumb as some of the things he's said or done himself...whether it's true or not.

When you trip and fall, a friend won't judge you or remark about how you should watch where you step. She'll just help you back to your feet, no questions asked.

A friend won't laugh at you, judge you, or make you feel inferior. He'll do what he can to shield you from embarrassment, cushion your fall, and help you clean up the messes in life.

Why do friends do all this? Because they know that's how they'd want us to treat them if they were in our shoes.

When you trip and fall, a friend won't judge you or remark about how you should watch where you step.

Do to others what you would have them do to you.

—Matthew 7:12

Friendship is born at the moment

when one person says to another,

"What?! You too!

Thought I was the only one."

C. S. Lewis

The best time to make friends is before you need them.

Ethel Barrymore

Friends Are a Blessing from God

When I need a hug, I go to _____.

When I'm feeling down, I go to _____.

When I need encouragement, I go to _____.

When I need prayer, I go to _____.

When I need a laugh, I go to _____.

When I need advice, I go to _____.

When I need stimulating conversation, I go to _____.

When I need a shoulder to lean on, I go to _____.

When I need help, I go to_____.

When I need all of the above, I go to_____.

Do not save your loving speeches

for your friends till they are dead.

Do not write them on their tombstones;

speak them rather now instead.

Anna Cummins

*You can keep in touch with your friends,
no matter where they are!*

THE where OF friendship

You can simply walk to your friend's house and say hello.

> **Wherever you are,
> it is your own friends who make your world.**

Ralph B. Perry

Near, Far, Wherever You Are

Years ago, it was more difficult to keep in touch with friends. You either had to send a telegram or write a letter and send it by messenger, hoping and praying that he didn't get killed along the way.

Today, we have available to us just about every means of communication. We still have the telegram and messenger services, but we also have the telephone, e-mail, first-class mail, priority mail, express mail, cell phones, and pagers. We can keep in touch with friends no matter how many miles apart we happen to be. We can drive a car, ride a motorcycle or scooter, hop on a horse, or even use the old fashioned means of travel—walking—to go over to a friend's house and say hello.

Distance between friends is no longer an excuse for not staying in touch. Since moving to Tennessee from California, I communicate with some friends a lot more than I ever did when they lived only a few miles from me. We live in a great time for friendships.

But e-mails don't write themselves. The telephone can do a lot of things, but it can't pick itself up and dial a number for us. We have to press the right keys. We have to make the phone call or send the e-mail. We have to put forth the effort. But friends are worth it.

Can miles truly separate us from friends?
If we want to be with someone we love,
aren't we already there?

Richard Bach

Go oft to the house of thy friend,

for weeds choke the unused path.

Ralph Waldo Emerson

I have lost friends, some by death,
others through sheer inability to cross the street.

Virginia Woolf

A friendship can weather most things and thrive in thin soil—
but it needs a little mulch of letters and phone calls
and small silly presents every so often—
just to save it from drying out completely.

Pam Brown

There is no distance too far between friends,
for friendship gives wings to the heart.

Kathy Kay Benudiz

A true friend is someone who is there for you when they would rather be someplace else.

Len Wein

Friends Are There for Us

Have you ever wondered where you would be without your friends? If you have, you know it's a place you wouldn't ever want to be. Friends mean the world to us. Over the years, they've encouraged us, laughed with us, cried with us, and prayed with us. Some friends have been in our lives since childhood; others are new friends we've only recently come to know. But whether we've known them for years or only months, one thing's for certain—life is a lot fuller because of the friends who happen to be in it.

Friends are our stability, our peace, our comfort in difficult times, and our joy in good times. We all need good friends. Friends we can count on. Friends who have stood the test of time. Without friends, who would we call as our lifeline when we're going for the big money on *Who Wants to Be a Millionaire*? Without friends, who would get excited for us if someday we just happen to win a Pulitzer Prize or get an honorable mention in the annual chili cook-off at the state fair? Without friends, who would we talk to while we're nervously awaiting the laboratory results from our latest medical test? Friends—the faithful and true kind—are life's golden nuggets. They may be hard to find, but once we find them, we're rich by any standard.

Without friends, who would get excited if we get an honorable mention in the annual chili cook-off?

**It's not where you go or what you do,
it's who you take along with you.**

Anonymous

Where'd Everybody Go?

Have you ever found yourself in a difficult situation where you could have used the support of your friends, but when you looked around for them, they were nowhere to be found?

Noah found himself in that kind of predicament. God told him to build an ark because he was going to send a flood to destroy the world. Being the obedient man of God that he was, Noah complied. And what happened? Did his friends and neighbors offer to assist him in this noble cause? Did they stop by with a fried-chicken dinner? A casserole? Did they nominate him Man of the Year at the annual homeowners' association meeting?

No. In fact, they did just the opposite. They laughed at him.

"What's Noah building now?"

"He says it's some kind of ark."

"An ark? Why does he need an ark out here? We're miles from the nearest water. I tell ya, Maggie, the guy's losing it!"

Apparently, Noah's friends and neighbors weren't very loyal. Not one of them stood up for Noah and said, "Hey, this is Noah we're talking about. He's a good man. He's never done anything like this before. Maybe we should listen to what he's saying. Maybe there really is going to be a flood."

Siding with Noah would have meant being ostracized from the rest of the neighborhood, and no one was willing to do that—friend or not. So they laughed, and they all turned a deaf ear to Noah's doom-and-gloom warning.

It must have hurt Noah's feelings more than a little to realize that the people he had waved to every morning, the neighbors he had chatted with, the men he had seen working in their fields every spring, would rather risk drowning than stand by him and his "ridiculous" new woodworking project.

So Noah and his family stood alone. They stood alone as they built the ark. They stood alone as they loaded it with two of every kind of animal. And they were still standing alone inside the ark when God's hand shut the door and the rains came and drowned all the skeptics.

Sometimes it really pays to believe in your friends.

Did Noah's friends stop by with a fried-chicken dinner?
No. They laughed at him.

Friendship is a sheltering tree.

Samuel Taylor Coleridge

Shelter in the Storm

Once while my family and I were visiting Disney World in Florida in the hot and humid month of August, a midafternoon rain shower hit without a lot of warning. I've never seen rain come down like that. The clouds must have dropped at least a half-inch of rain in less than fifteen minutes.

People ran for shelter wherever they could find it—in the stores, on the rides, under the table umbrellas in the dining areas. Our family and about ten other people took cover under a nearby tree. It was a large tree with far-reaching limbs and a full spray of leaves that formed a perfect protective canopy. Under that tree, it didn't really matter how hard it was raining or how alarmed we were each time we saw Mickey Mouse floating by. We stayed safe and dry.

Friends can be like that tree. When one of life's unexpected downpours hits, our friends can provide a canopy of protection for us. If we let them, they can be our shelter, our shield, and our safe haven until the storm passes.

Friends are a safe haven until the storm passes by.

Sticks in a bundle are unbreakable,

sticks alone can be broken by a child.

✿
Rabbi Marc Gellman

A friend may well be reckoned the masterpiece of nature.

✿
Ralph Waldo Emerson

Friends keep us from
being all alone.

THE why OF friendship

Laughter has been proven to boost the immune system
—even burn off calories.

Good friends are good for your health.

Irwin Sarason

The Friendship Diet

That's right. Forget that blue plate liver special, the bran muffins, tofu sandwiches, and even those alfalfa-sprout smoothies.

Our close friendships could very well be doing our bodies just as much good as health food. There are lots of reasons for this. One might be that good friends tend to laugh a lot when they get together—and laughter has been proven to boost the immune system, release mood-adjusting endorphins, and even burn off calories. Some choice, huh? Meet your best friend at Starbucks and laugh for an hour, or go to the gym and work out on the treadmill for an hour. Hmmm…let's see. Which sounds like more fun?

Another thing friends do when they get together is talk. They open up; share their struggles; admit their fears, faults, and confusion; and allow themselves to be vulnerable with each other. Medical science has long acknowledged the danger of keeping things bottled up inside us. Friends are therapeutic.

Friends also help each other, and there are many benefits to that. Friends encourage, advise, support, and defend. They commiserate, pray—they do whatever they can to make the other person's burdens a little lighter. And when you help someone else, you feel better about yourself.

The best mirror is an old friend.

George Herbert

We need old friends to help us grow

and new friends to keep us young.

✿

Letty C. Rayhobis

Treasure the love you receive above all.

It will survive long after your good health has vanished.

✿

Og Mandino

Friends broaden our horizons.

They serve as new models with whom we can identify.

They allow us to be ourselves—and accept us that way.

They enhance our self-esteem because they think we're OK—

because we matter to them.

✿

Judith Viorst

Why We Need Friends

Without friends to laugh with,

WE BECOME TOO SERIOUS.

Without friends to talk to,

WE BECOME TOO INTROSPECTIVE.

Without friends to cry with,

WE BECOME COLD AND INDIFFERENT.

Without friends to work with,

WE BECOME NEGATIVE AND SELF-PITYING.

Without friends to listen to,

WE BECOME SELF-ABSORBED.

Without friends to care about,

WE BECOME APATHETIC.

Without friends to share new adventures,

WE BECOME BORING.

Without friends to call or visit,

WE BECOME RECLUSIVE.

Without friends to hold us accountable,

WE BECOME TOO
SELF-RELIANT—
AND WE FAIL.

Without friends,

WE BECOME UNFRIENDLY.

Friends help us become a better us!

If a man does not make new acquaintances as he advances through life,

he will soon find himself left alone;

one should keep his friendships in constant repair.

Samuel Johnson

It's so much more friendly

with two.

Piglet (in *Winnie the Pooh,* by A. A. Milne)

The person who tries to live alone will not succeed as a human being.

His heart withers if it does not answer another heart.

His mind shrinks away if he hears only the echoes

of his own thoughts and finds no other inspiration.

Pearl S. Buck

> **Never refuse any advance of friendship, for if nine out of ten bring you nothing, one alone may repay you.**
>
>
>
> **Madame de Tencin**

Even Jesus Needed Friends

Jesus knew the importance of having friends. Matthew, Mark, Luke, John, and the others He spent much of His time with were more than mere disciples of His teaching. They were His friends. He ate with them, traveled with them, laughed with them, and discussed spiritual matters with them—many of the same things we do with our friends.

Jesus even knows what it feels like to lose a friend. Lazarus was such a good friend that Jesus wept openly when He heard that Lazarus had died. Jesus raised him from the dead, and even though the miracle was to glorify God, can you imagine the reunion they had when Lazarus walked out of that tomb?

Jesus also knows what it feels like to be pulled into a competition of sorts between two friends. One day Martha complained to Jesus that she was doing all the work while her sister Mary just sat around at Jesus' feet. If you've ever been in the middle of one friend complaining about another, you know what an uncomfortable position that can be. Jesus handled it well, though, basically telling Martha to relax and enjoy His presence. He knew she was doing most, if not all, of the work; but what Mary was doing was important too.

Jesus knows what it feels like to be betrayed by a friend. Judas, a friend He loved, sold Him out for only thirty pieces of silver. We know that Jesus' death and resurrection were in God's plan, but it still had to hurt Jesus when His "friend" Judas was revealed to be His betrayer.

When it comes to friendship, Jesus knows a lot about it. He knows the ups and downs, the joys and the pain. He knows how much we all need our friends. And on the cross, He proved Himself to be our truest friend of all.

> *Greater love has no one than this, that he lay down his life for his friends.*
>
> —John 15:13

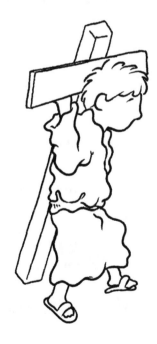

To laugh often and much; to win the respect of intelligent people

and the affection of children; to earn the appreciation of honest

critics and endure the betrayal of false friends;

to appreciate beauty, to find the best in others;

to leave the world a little better; whether by a healthy child,

a garden patch, or a redeemed social condition;

to know even one life has breathed easier because you have lived.

This is the meaning of success.

Ralph Waldo Emerson

Just when you think that a person

is just a backdrop for the rest of the universe,

watch them and see that they laugh, they cry,

they tell jokes...they're just friends waiting to be made.

Jeffrey Borenstein

Friends know how to lift us up when we're feeling down.

THE how OF friendship

If only our schools would teach classes on friendship…

> **The only way to have a friend is to be one.**
>
>
>
> **Ralph Waldo Emerson**

Friendship 101

The world would be a better place if only our schools would teach classes on friendship. Too many of us don't know how to be good friends. That could be for a lot of different reasons. Maybe we're too busy to take the time necessary to build good friendships. Maybe we're too self-focused and see our own needs to the exclusion of the needs of our friends. Maybe we've never had a good example of friendship. Or maybe we're not good friends to others because we're not good friends to ourselves.

Being a good friend means loving unconditionally. Friendship isn't a carrot to be dangled in front of others and pulled away every time they do something we don't like. Friendship is love without requirements and loyalty without stipulations.

Being a good friend also requires a sacrifice of time. We're all busy. We're all overcommitted. We've all got family, church, work, and civic duties. But our friendships need our time and attention too; otherwise, they'll die. You wouldn't expect to keep your job if you never showed up for work—or your position on a church or civic committee if you never fulfilled those responsibilities. These commitments require our time, and we understand that. Friendship requires time too.

Friendship is a lot of work. If it were easy, friends wouldn't be so valuable. Building and maintaining a friendship is something that requires a lot of effort, a lot of energy, and a lot of dedication.

Being a good friend requires selflessness as well. Sometimes we might have to do without a new video we've been wanting so we can surprise our friend with the new CD she's been wanting.

True friendship is more than lip service. It requires a lot from us, but if we do it right, we'll reap a lifetime of rewards.

You don't just luck into things as much as you'd like to think you do.
You build step by step, whether it's friendships or opportunities.

Barbara Bush

If we would build on a sure foundation in friendship,
we must love friends for their sake rather than for our own.

Charlotte Brontë

We secure our friends not by accepting favors,
but by doing them.

Thucydides

The ABCs of Friendship

Friends Appreciate

I keep my friends as misers do their treasure,
because, of all the things granted us by wisdom,
none is greater or better than friendship.

Pietro Aretino

Friends Believe

The glory of friendship is not in the outstretched hand,
nor the kindly smile, nor the joy of companionship;
it is in the spiritual inspiration that comes to one when he
discovers that someone else believes in him
and is willing to trust him.

Ralph Waldo Emerson

Friends Care

The friend who can be silent
with us in a moment of despair or confusion,
who can stay with us in an hour of grief
and bereavement, who can tolerate
not knowing, not curing, not healing
and face with us the reality
of our powerlessness,
that is a friend who cares.

Henri Nouwen

Friends Defend

**Be true to your work, your
word, and your friend.**

Henry David Thoreau

Friends Encourage

**A man never likes you so well
as when he leaves your company liking himself.**

Anonymous

Friends Forgive

**Two persons cannot long be friends
if they cannot forgive each other's little failings.**

Jean De La BruyFre

Friends Give

Every gift from a friend
is a wish for your happiness.

Richard Bach

Friends Help

We do not so much need the help
of our friends as the confidence
of their help in need.

Epicurus

Friends Inspire

Friends show me what I can do.

Johann Friedrich Von Schiller

Friends Joke

That is the best–to laugh with someone
because you think the same things are funny.

Jean De La BruyFre

Friends Kneel
Friends, please pray for us.

1 Thessalonians 5:25 CEV

Friends Listen
You can make more friends in two months
by becoming really interested in other people
than you can in two years by trying to get other people
interested in you.

Dale Carnegie

Friends Maximize and Minimize

Friendship doubles our joy and divides our grief.

Swedish proverb

Friends Nurture

**Treat people as if they were what they ought to be,
and you help them to become what they are capable of being.**

Johann Wolfgang von Goethe

Friends Overlook

A true friend is one who overlooks your failures and tolerates your success.

Doug Larson

Friends Protect

Do not protect yourself by a fence, but rather by your friends.

Czech proverb

Friends Question

If all my friends were
to jump off a bridge,
I wouldn't jump with them;
I'd be at the bottom
to catch them.

Tim McGraw

Friends Remember

No distance of place or lapse of time can lessen
the friendship of those who are thoroughly
persuaded of each other's worth.

Robert Southey

Friends Sacrifice

**It is not what you give your friend,
but what you are *willing* to give him
that determines the quality of friendship.**

Mary Dixon Thayer

Friends Talk

There was a definite process by which one made people into friends, and it involved talking to them and listening to them for hours at a time.

❀

Rebecca West

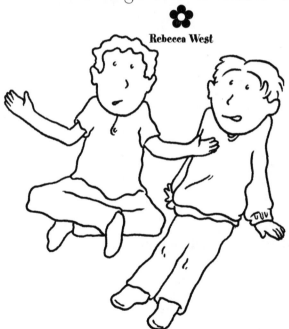

Friends Uplift

Friendship is a strong and habitual inclination in two persons to promote the good and happiness of one another.

Eustace Budgell

Friends Validate

The greatest good you can do for another is not just to share your riches but to reveal to him his own.

Benjamin Disraeli

Friends Welcome

Stay is a charming word in a friend's vocabulary.

Louisa May Alcott

Friends eXhort

Reprove thy friend privately; commend him publicly.

Solon

Friends Yield

To be loved, be lovable.

Ovid

Friends "Zip It"

Don't flatter yourself that friendship authorizes you to say disagreeable things to your intimates. The nearer you come into relation with a person, the more necessary do tact and courtesy become. Except in cases of necessity, which are rare, leave your friend to learn unpleasant things from his enemies; they are ready enough to tell them.

Oliver Wendell Holmes

The best kind of friend

is the kind you can sit on a porch swing with,

never say a word, then walk away feeling like it was

the best conversation that you ever had.

Anonymous

Treat your friends as you do your best pictures,
and place them in their best light.

Jennie Jerome Churchill

Blessed are they who have the gift of making friends,

for it is one of God's best gifts. It involves many things,

but above all, the power of going out of one's self

and appreciating whatever is noble and loving in another.

Thomas Hughes

Lessons from Man's Best Friend

Dogs teach us that...
Loyalty is everything.

Dogs are inherently loyal. They've been known to stay by their masters' sides long after their masters die, sometimes even to the point of sacrificing their own lives. Why? Because when dogs love, they do it for life. If you hurt their feelings, they won't scratch your name out of their address book. Relationships mean more to them than that. A dog won't turn his back on someone he's close to, no matter how many times you've accidentally stepped on his tail.

Love is unconditional.

Dogs love you no matter what. They won't giggle behind your back when your barber cuts your hair too  short. They'll admire you even if you get passed over for that promotion at work. A dog will jump up on your lap and lick your face even after you've shooed him away time and time again. A dog's love has little to do with your looks or your successes or failures. Dogs just love you for being you.

You shouldn't bark at those who love you most.

Dogs understand this unwritten rule—you don't growl at, bark at, or bite your friends. Simple rule, but we humans sometimes forget it.

Words aren't always necessary
to show someone you care.

Dogs don't speak English. Or German. Or French, for that matter. They don't have e-mail or cell phones or pagers. They can't send greeting cards or flowers to show they care. They can't even smile—at least, not like we do. But do dogs let any of this stop them from showing love? No. They express their love in lots of different ways. They know instinctively—and we should too—that actions speak a whole lot louder than words.

Life is more fun when you play.

Dogs understand the importance of playtime. They also know that fetching, catching a Frisbee, or even playing with chew toys is a lot more fun when two participate. Or three. Or more. Friends and fun just go together!

When you're with your best friend,
even running around in circles can be fun.

Dogs know you don't have to spend a fortune to have a good time. When you're with your best friend, something as simple as running around in circles can be as exciting as visiting the Leaning Tower of Pisa. And with my sense of direction, running around in circles is something my friends and I do a lot!

Outside of a dog, a book is a man's best friend.

Inside a dog it's too dark to read.

Groucho Marx

Lessons from a Girl's Best Friend

Diamonds teach us that...
A little dirt doesn't change your worth.

None of us will get through life without having a little dirt kicked on us. Whether the dirt is from our own doing or kicked on us by others, the presence of dirt doesn't change our value. All we need is a friend to come along and help us clean it off, and our worth will come shining through again.

GROAN

Good things can come from pressure.

Without pressure, diamonds wouldn't even exist. Carbon endures tremendous amounts of pressure before it becomes a diamond. It's not easy, but the result is amazing. So next time a relationship seems too hard and you're ready to give up, remember that pressure is how valuable diamonds—and priceless friendships—are formed.

Just as iron sharpens iron,
friends sharpen the minds
of each other.

—Proverbs 27:17 CEV

Life is to be fortified by many friendships.

To love and to be loved

is the greatest happiness of existence.

Sydney Smith

Ta da!

THE
last word
ON
friendship

Friends Are Forever

If we're lucky, our lives will be blessed with the kinds of friends who not only stay in our address books day after day, month after month, and year after year, but stay in our hearts as well. They stay through the fun times and the difficult times too. They stay in spite of whatever miles may lie between us. They stay through the misunderstandings and all those busy times when communication, though well intentioned, is minimal. They stay because they cherish the friendship as much as we do. Friends like this deserve to be saluted. This book is our way of doing just that.

Friends who stay deserve to be saluted.

The Ten Commandments of Friendship

1. **Thou shalt not hesitate to call your friend at any hour of the day or night in the event of an emergency. Or a moonlight-madness sale.**

2. Thou shalt never turn your back on a friend—especially if there's a slice of tiramisu in front of you.

3. Thou shalt overlook your friend's imperfections as your friend (whether you realize it or not) has daily overlooked yours.

4. Thou shalt trust your friend, and your friend shall always prove worthy of that trust.

5. Thou shalt defend your friend with the same fervor you would want him or her to display defending you.

6. Thou shalt always be ready to laugh, cry, celebrate, commiserate, dream, plan, and eat chocolate-chip ice cream with your friend.

7. Thou shalt communicate with your friend as often as possible by whatever means available to you—telephone, letter, e-mail, stone tablet, hot-air balloon, or note in a bottle.

8. Thou shalt forgive a friend seventy times seven. With true friends there are no "last straws."

9. **Thou shalt not become a disappearing act when your friend is behaving at his or her worst, for this is when he or she needs your friendship most.**

10. Thou shalt appreciate a friend, for a friend is a person who loves you not only unconditionally but totally by choice.

Friend Extraordinaire!

❀ Friendship Certification ❀

Howard University hereby awards the title of

Friend Extraordinaire

to

_____

for having exhibited the qualities of true friendship to

_____

This award is presented on

the _____ day of _____, in the year _____.

_____

President of Howard University of Friendship

❀ Friendship Coupon ❀

The bearer of this coupon is entitled to one guilt-free dessert.
(Disclaimer: Coupon doesn't actually remove calories from the dessert.
It simply prohibits any discussion of the calories.)

✿ Friendship Coupon ✿

The bearer of this coupon is entitled to
one friendship outing without the
interruption of a single cell-phone call.

✿ Friendship Coupon ✿

The bearer of this coupon is entitled
to one afternoon of shopping
with friends, whether anything is
purchased or not.

✿ Friendship Coupon ✿

The bearer of this coupon is entitled to
receive one free pass on a
foot-in-the-mouth comment.

✿ Friendship Coupon ✿

The bearer of this coupon is
guaranteed a shoulder to lean on when
standing becomes too difficult.

✿ Friendship Coupon ✿

The bearer of this coupon is
guaranteed one friendship hug
whenever necessary.

✿ Friendship Coupon ✿

The bearer of this coupon is entitled to
an emergency hour of laughter
and frivolous conversation
when life feels too serious.

Friendship Hall of Fame

Whereas _____ has cheerfully answered my calls at all hours of the day and night, never once using the Caller ID against me;

Has never let my dish at a church potluck go unsampled, but would faithfully risk life and gastrointestinal health to be the first person to take a scoop;

Has given me advice when I needed to hear it and has refrained from doing so when I just needed to be heard;

Has provided endless encouragement during my darkest hours;

And has always been there to laugh with me, even when I felt least like doing so;

Whereas _____ has always believed in me;

Has been the same friend both behind my back and to my face;

And has gone above and beyond the call of friendship time and time and time again;

_____ **is hereby inducted into the Friendship Hall of Fame.**

The End

Look for these other *"Official"* books:
The "Official" Hugs Book
The "Official" Grad Book